Nirvana:

Pieces of Self-Healing II

Dedication

Here's an open letter from the bottom of my heart to my supporters. I love you all, genuinely. The words of affirmations, messages, and pictures you send fills my heart with the fuel that keeps me going. When I have my moments of doubt, wondering if I'm doing enough, or I'll be just another great writer who will get overlooked in his lifetime, someone comes to mute those voices that lingers in my head with support. Without you all I would have probably given up long ago. It feels good to know my words are helping my others, but the words and stories I receive everyday has helped me more than anyone can fathom. This journey has led me to connect with some of the most beautiful souls from close and far, young and old. The diversity of my audience is truly special. I love how I'm accepted as myself - the man, and writer - and you all still can relate to and appreciate

my message. We have a special bond. ❤ ❤ ❤ . There are dozens, maybe hundreds of writers (especially poets) who are far more 'popular' than I am, but that didn't cloud your judgement, nor did it stop you from using your hard-earned money to purchase my book(s) and allowing it to have a huge impact on you. It shows how special of a human you are, because in today's climate of poetry where popularity is more important than talent (to most consumers) you didn't let that stop you from buying, supporting, and boosting my work. I appreciate that fact you all appreciate my fiction writing just as much too. I've come so far since my first release in 2013 but I have even longer to go.

I know I may come off as cocky and self-boasting, but I'm well-aware that would not have come this far without any of you.

Thank you so much, I hope you all continue to support my work as I continue to document my journey.

With Love, Michael Tavon

Dedication II

To the love of my life, Moonsoulchild. you're everything I could ever ask for in a woman. Your love has lifted me to newer heights. When self-doubt gets me down, you lift me up with affirmations and warmth. Your passion matches mine. I love you with every inch of my heart and from the depth of my spirit. Thank you for being my friend, lover, light, and love.

Michael Tavon

The Pieces

Piece One

For Sara,
To the perfect stranger from afar
Who has yielded more support
Than those closest to me
your heart beats hard enough
To shift mountains
Yet still holds the softness of a raindrop
In an industry filled with ego maniacs,
manipulators, and users
I've found you, a writer who supports without
an agenda
A human with a humble spirit
And a woman with words that's genuine
I appreciate you honestly
Truly your soul is filled with inspiration
That you pour into the world
And I thank you for being you
I thank you for understanding
As I can say without a doubt
You are my first true author friend

Dated 5/6/18

Piece Two

11 more days: after we finish this marathon.
After we cross the finish line. We'll finally begin
our forever together. I've learned to appreciate
this wait. I've falling in love with the distance.
You're worth every minute spent waiting.
You're worth every mile traveled. My heart is so
open for you. My love is overflowing.
Everything about our love, our relationship has
been done right, distance and time, set our
foundation, nothing is knocking us down.
We've learned to love each other with little
physical contact. I feel your heart beating for me
when I pray, that's how connected we are. Time
and distance tested our will, our patience, and
loyalty. No temptation was strong enough to
tear our bond apart. Here we are as happy as
ever. Yes, some nights were harder than others.
When I yearn to roll over and caress your inner
thigh and you're not there I'm struck by
disappointment then I dream of us making trips
to the grocery store, making out at concerts and
exploring the world.

I wake up with joy knowing soon we'll be together, face to face, every night for the rest of our lives.

Dated 7/30/18

<u>Piece Three</u>

To give the most fragile parts of you
To a person who was once a stranger
Is the bravest act a human could do
Which is why falling in love is scary as hell

<u>Piece Four</u>

From flirting to fucking
A seamless transition
We both knew, inevitable
What I didn't expect
Was how deeply I'd fallen
For you, after we climaxed

Piece Five

How procrastination works
"I'll do it tomorrow" turns into next week
Next week turns into next month
next month turns into a year
a year turns into eventually
Eventually becomes never
then never becomes too late
And too late turns into regret.

Piece Six

Some nights we FaceTime
And don't say much
Just the presence of our faces
Makes us feel less alone

Michael Tavon

Piece Seven

I've found a relationship with *happiness*
and we grow stronger each day
Even when I crawl back to *self-loathing*
Since *loneliness* was all I ever loved
happiness finds a way
to pull me out the dark hole
before I fall too deep
I broke up with *toxic thoughts*
and stopped flirting with fear,
now I rest easy, at night,
when joy sings in my ear.

<u>Piece Eight</u>

Thunder Storms blew off your petals
then you bloomed again
the soles of many shoes
crushed your stem
you came back stronger

Even when filthy hands
gripped around your base
you remained beautiful

As the life of a flower
the world will do everything
to crush you,
but you refuse to die
see, I must learn to admire
your radiance from a far

Appreciating you unconditionally
is what I'll do
even if that means
keeping my hands off your stem
and stepping off your soil

That's true love
and it's here in the way
that will help you bloom
into the best version of you

Piece Nine

The ink from your past
Left marks
You can't erase
So you dreadfully stare for countless hours
Wishing they would somehow vanish,
But they never do
They're apart of you
Til the day you rest breathless,
And it hurts me to see you
Wear misery like a tattoo,
Those tracings of pain
Will never fade
Years after the ink pen stops bleeding
You're stuck with that damn tattoo
Constantly reminding you
Of how much of a fool you once were
And that's okay
Can you say you really lived
If you've never made a mistake?
Can you really say you've grown without pain?

Hell no,

Nirvana: Pieces of Self-Healing II

So stop wasting precious time
Regretting that damn
Tattoo you got
On that drunken night.
or when you were young and dumb
Laugh it off
And make more mistakes
.... We all need more tattoos

Michael Tavon

Piece Ten

you're a star
don't allow the cloud
of *self-doubt*
to shroud your shine

Piece Eleven

too often we use sex as a tool
to feel less broken
hoping the temporary pleasure will fix
the damage inflicted by our haunting mistakes
fifteen minutes of bliss
ends with a kiss
and a half-empty bed
A sad cycle of lust and disappoint
that leaves us more hopeless
than we were before.
it's time to stop running from pain
by trying to find ways to cope with being alone

Piece Twelve

Happiness is on the other side
Of a frozen brick wall
expanding along the border
Of my brain
All I own is a rusty chisel
And a hammer
I chip away
piece by piece
inch by inch
until I feel it breaking through
in the midst of an ice cold hell
My thoughts remain
Warm and strong
My will refuses to give up
My body refuses to die
The process is fraught
But the thought of making
It to their side
Gives me peace

<u>Piece Thirteen</u>

to the flame
who sparks the wild embers
in my iris
when you smile
I can't contain my flame
so I gaze from afar
to admire your beauty and rage

my flame
forever changing hues
to match your passionate moods

what can I do to get you to notice me
'cause when I touch you
I receive third degree.

since I can't hold you close
I'll watch you grow

in the distance in an instant
you spread without assistance
you don't need permission

as you turn your past into ashes
allowing new life to form

Michael Tavon

Our love rises
I'm finally without sadness

I'm happy to watch
our fire bloom
this fire is too wild
to burn out soon

<u>Piece Fourteen</u>

"Am I good enough?"
"Am I worth it?"
I ask self-doubt as she lays
On her side of the bed, half nude,
blowing smoke to the ceiling.
"I've had better," she smiles.
The truth gashes through my skin
like a scythe.

I turnover,
she caresses my back
This dirty affair we share is fun to her
but taxing to my energy.
She loves my company,
Because I'm miserable too.

I love who I am when I'm alone
But somehow, I feel less than myself
when she's around.
I guess I've found comfort
In disappointing myself
It's 3 am and my body is worn.

Michael Tavon

I spent the entire night
expanding my energy,
in hopes of her falling in love with my effort.

When I fall short
of her impossible expectations
I go for another round
and another until she gets tired
I'm drained
She'll never be satisfied.

When she leaves tonight
I'll change the locks this time
which doesn't matter,
I'll probably give her the key again.

Piece Fifteen

As she lays on her stomach
Feet crossed,
Earphones plugged in
Writing a lengthy piece on her phone

I spot the
Acne dotted across her back shoulders
Strands of loose hair all over the bedspread
The dimples above her ass and
stretchmarks on the side of her cheeks

"She's more beautiful when naked"
I think to myself

She's so free
Her insecurities, her flaws
She lets 'em all out
When she's with me.
Her naked soul, and nude body
Stretched across the sheets
She's so beautiful
When comfortable

And I'm in love with this type of energy
I'm so lucky to see her naked.

Piece Sixteen

When I'm with her
Fear
Anxiety
And excuses
Take their baggage
And vacate to St. Elsewhere
Leaving me to be
the best version of myself for her.
While they're away
I'm at peace, without fear
Knowing she's here, in my ear
Driving me to get my shit together.
As the master of procrastination
I need that motivation
She cleans the dirt from my heart
She cuts the rope that's holding me back.
She saves me from harming myself

Piece Seventeen

Cry, but stay strong
Let those tears flow
While holding your head high
pain doesn't break you
it shapes you.

Piece Eighteen

"You're soft but not easily open,
this why I'm drawn to you"
this was said by a woman
I've have yet to meet I person
she lives a thousand miles away
that line made me pause, I thought
"This goes to show we're far more than our
physical presence."

to leave a deep impression on a stranger
who you only contact via direct message
is devine and pure
to me its means
our spirits are far stronger
than our physical being

we connect without seeing eye to eye
we feel each other without a gentle touch
that's a spiritual connection
damn, I love social media

(this was written before Sara an I met for the
first time)

Piece Nineteen

You took the pain of feeling unwanted and made it disappear. The world's greatest act. You reached through my chest and opened my heart again. You opened my eyes now I believe in magic like I'm a child for the second time. Your love makes me feel invincible.

(The text I sent before asking her to be my woman)

Piece Twenty

Last night
You cried on my chest
Because you fear your imperfections
Will drive me away
I grabbed your face and kissed your wet cheeks
and said, "baby I didn't fall in love you
because I thought you were perfect."

Then you discovered we share the same fear
I fear one day you will wake up
and feel that I'm not enough for you.

We kissed with a reassuring passion
And slow danced to "Anytime" by Ray J
In the dark for thirty minutes.

During a night
nothing went as planned
it rained,
the food sucked,
the cover band was awful,
your sister was being a bitch,
and I had a massive headache that prevented us
from making love, at first.

Yet we somehow ended it with the most
intimate moment we ever shared.
We experienced an emotional climax
We sang the lyrics to each other
Then made wild love.

Piece Twenty-one

It took a while for me to love myself
the learning process
was filled with many trials and tribulations
fake smiles and empty laughs

Many days I convinced myself I was fine
by numbing my pain
with delusions of grandeur
after inhaling
smoke from weed blunts
and quenching my thirst
with whiskey shots

"I'm happy," I lied to myself hundreds of times.
"I love myself," I tried to convince my mind.
 while deep inside I was fighting for peace
 the biggest battle I had to overcome,
 but the first step I had to take
 was accepting my sadness,
 and finding ways to defeat it.

The battle became a war,
but I survived the crossfire
now I'm a warrior,
and a person
who learned to love
everything within

Piece Twenty-two

The love of a broken man
Is intense when he finds the right one
Because he'll do everything in his power
To make sure his lover never feels the pain
He went through in his past life.

Piece Twenty-three

My doubts, my fears, and insecurities
are all in the rearview, because of you
I removed memory lane from of my route,
I see vividly with you in my present
I only wish to move forward with you while
taking our time.

<u>Piece Twenty-four</u>

Depression is the ex who tries to creep
back into your life
when they see you doing fine,
begging to get back into
your heart one last time.
They text
"Do you miss me?"
"Hey stranger."
Bring up old memories
to put you back into your misery.
then they visit your mother's home
every Sunday
knowing someday you'll drop by to say hey.
When you finally move on to another love
whether it be yourself
or someone else
ex-depression has a way of testing
your strength
by pulling out every desperate attempt
in hopes of you crawling back to them.
Most of us fail this test,
because we're too scared to move on,
but you gotta stay strong
to be happy, please move on
tell depression to fuck off

Piece Twenty-five

I was enslaved by sadness
For so long,
it's going to take a while to adjust
to being free .
Happiness is here.
I can be myself without
the shackles and chains.
My mind is at peace
I'm in love with this feeling
I'll do whatever it takes
to keep going

Sadness is the past
I'm free at last
the love I have for myself
is too strong to run back

I chased happiness for so long
it finally met me halfway
it was worth the effort
I'll do it all over again
the same exact way
for this feeling
is mine, no one has the power to take it away

Piece Twenty-six

children,
I tell them to wait to grow up
time only ruins you.
stay pure, remain gold
for as long as possible
being an adult means
being a slave to responsibilities
heartache and mental breakdowns
so tell your children
to stay young
remain free and patient

Piece Twenty-seven

This is for my brothers who are too afraid to cry

This for my brothers who think breaking down

Is a sign of weakness

Your heart isn't made of iron

Suppressed feelings turn to rage

Sit down, and cry

It's okay to feel

Stop cramming those emotions

inside a glass jar

Because once it cracks

You will lose all control of yourself

And that what society wants

Another 'crazy' brother

Another brother they can depict as a misfit

Remember, soldiers cry too

<u>Piece Twenty-eight</u>

Before you I thought
it was impossible to love me
women treated my affection like an infection
and protected their hearts out of fear
I was 'too much' or 'not enough'
those were the excuses they used
as I became more vulnerable
and my mystery faded
they vanished into thin air
I was falling for magicians the whole time
then came you.
eager to fall into my arms
I fooled myself into thinking
you were another woman allured
by the mystery you saw in me
and once I opened my trust
you were going to shut the door
as if you saw a monster on the other side
I put my guard up,
but you kept jabbing at my defense
until your persistence penetrated through
my chest of steel

Piece Twenty-nine

I realized how easy it was to love
and how easy it was for me to be loved.
you've helped me see
that I was more than a temporary fling
because you saw forever in my stare.
Thank you for being bold
enough to love me,
thank you for believing
in my heart.

<u>Piece Thirty</u>

You took a leap
rock bottom
you landed
it hurts
you're embarrassed
bruised
damaged,
but now you're
stronger
wiser
fearless
a survivor
tragedy turns to growth
when you let it

Piece Thirty-one

Life is like a diner
In which you ask
"What's the special?"
The server says
"Today its Honey Glazed Doubt, (recommended
temp well-done) with your choice of steamed
procrastination, sautéed self-loathing, or
mashed scattered thoughts as the side.
You pass on the enticing meal, glance at the
menu.
And ask, 'drink specials?'
Yes! We have bottomless anxiety, and irrational
red fear"
"I'll just have water with lemon" you respond.
The server stands with a grin as you continue to
scan the menu.
Your face lights up when your eyes glance upon
something appealing.
"What about the happiness with a side of love?"
You wonder.
"Oh, that's a good one...well-done or medium?"
You take another glance at the menu and notice
something missing.
"What's the price?"

The server jots on the notepad, rips the sheet
and places it in front of you. You slowly tilt your
head down. Then look at your date, you wanna
leave, but afraid of looking broke, so to save face
You hesitate, pretend to contemplate, then say,
"I'll take the special"

Piece Thirty-two

After the long week
your body deserves extra care
It's tense from the stress
The world has caused
So lay on your chest,
Undress,
Relax your shoulders
As I reach for the castor oil
And dim the lights too
Tonight my hands will
get intimate with your skin
Caressing every inch
Causing your legs to sensually twitch
From your shoulders to back
to shoulders
I kiss your neck and whisper
Sweet everything's in your ear
You smile as your eyes close
you soak in the pleasure
You've been longing for
You're a queen
You deserve every minute and more
I let that be known
When I kiss those cheeks

Nirvana: Pieces of Self-Healing II

as I stroke the creases with my thumbs
You moan softly
As my hands dig deep
Soothing music provides
pleasure to our ears
The room smells
like the lavender candle that's burning
My hands slide down
To your thighs
I suck on those
Before I go to your toes
I run your feet until
The kinks are out
Anything for you, babe
No need to thank me, because you deserve this
No need to thank me
This pleases me as much as it pleases you

Piece Thirty-three

It's funny, we have to pursue happiness, but misery comes to us naturally. We work our entire lives to find something that may never appear.

~ better than not trying

<u>Piece Thirty-four</u>

To have someone who loves every piece of
you, unconditionally is the warmest, scariest,
and most peaceful feeling in the world.

Piece Thirty-five

These thoughts are a series of ferocious waves
crashing onto a rocky shore. They're majestic,
dark, and difficult to maintain. You've come into
my life and soothed the high tides. Thank you
for giving me a peace of mind.

<u>Piece Thirty-six</u>

Letting go of the old me was the hardest thing I had to do. Learning how to be more accountable for my own hurt, reprogramming my broken mindset, and self-doubt were things I had to overcome so I could grow into the best version of me.

Piece Thirty-seven

Growing up,
I thought real love was drunk nights
and verbal fights.
silent newspaper readings
chain smoking
plates of grits and bacon
and living distantly under the same roof

aunts and uncles
who never hugged or kissed their spouse
as if they were ashamed to show affection
and two parents who procreated
three children, but were emotionally numb
to each other.

so, I thought love was
fucking
punching
drinking
& dying

a sad reality for a kid
who loved to dream
about a different kind of love
even then
I knew that wasn't the 'love' for me

Piece Thirty-eight

pressuring yourself to be perfect
is a recipe for depression.
setting unrealistic expectations
upon yourself will send
your self-esteem spiraling
like a tornado.

as a human it's your birthright
to try and fail
you deserve to learn from your mistakes
give yourself the chance to
grow through your failures

keep failing upwards
continue to push forward
inch by inch
your goals will be met
just don't give up

Piece Thirty-nine

New experiences
brings out the child in me
A feeling I missed for years
Since moving to Connecticut I've seen
Wild deer,
A waterfall,
Camping grounds,
Heroin addicts
lost in a daze like zombie from
The Walking Dead,
My bipolar roommate explode,
Smelled skunk in the air,
Won $64 at the slots in the casino,
Made love five times in one night,
And twice every night since,
Moral of this story, if you get the chance to
move out of state or fall in love
Do it without hesitation
Don't wait to save money
or 'when the time is right'

Just do it set yourself free
I must say falling in love has paid off
Moving to a new state has inspired me
I feel like a child again
Happy and hopeful.

<u>Piece Forty</u>

I feel like there's a running joke that everyone is on but me. Here I am putting my heart into everything I write while I watch most of the top sellers recycle each other's themes and pieces. male poets writing cheap "she deserves better than him" type poetry and all the dry one-liners getting all the getting praised. It's all an easy way to get more shares, likes, and sales. I guess I'm the dumb one for actually trying.

Piece Forty-one

Damn, I fell in love

..Later that night
we got drunk off love
and played DVSN's *Morning After* album
through the speaker
we wrestled in the nude
til our eyes closed
I fell asleep, mid stroke inside of her
we discovered
two things
our love making was like two sparks
creating a flame
and for the first time
in what seemed like ages
I slept through an entire night without
waking up
her presence made me feel
safe from myself
because loneliness is a dangerous place
to visit when it's dark

Piece Forty-two

Lying to yourself
keeps you stuck
in the same place
you're dying to escape from.

The old saying
"the truth shall set you free"
is a cliché for a reason.

When you live a life of lies
you become a prisoner to your own mind
trying to maintain the facade you've created

with truth comes growth, wisdom,
and freedom.
To set yourself free
honestly is key.

Piece Forty-three

When you show how
Passionate you are
They will call you
Crazy,
Insane,
A dreamer with no sense of reality
I'll be all those things
Before I'd become a person
Who has given up
I'd rather be called crazy than a quitter

Piece Forty-four

Sometimes we disappoint ourselves by setting unrealistic expectations upon our love interests. We fetishize their potential instead of falling in love with who they truly are.

We often break our own hearts.

Piece Forty-five

I was seven years young
happily listening to one of my mixed CDs
until my favorite track
"what these bitches want" by DMX
began to skip

I rushed to the bathroom,
rubbed the cd with alcohol, water, peroxide
nothing worked

I ran to my father
"What do yo do when your favorite song
skips?"
"find another one," he shrugged.
I went back to my room
disappointed
thinking my father didn't care

years later I realized that was the best advice
he could've given, because that was first lesson I
learned about moving on.

<u>Piece Forty-six</u>

Happiness looks beautiful on you

Too bad life rarely has it in stock

And the price is ridiculous

So take care of the what you have

Hold on to it

Make it last for as long as you can

Without stains,

Tears,

Rips,

or shrinkage

Happiness fits you so well

You style it in so many ways

I wish you would wear it everyday,

But it's hard for us to stay the same

When life forces us to change

Piece Forty-seven

The way you pour your heart out
There no way you would
leave my glass half empty
I'll sip every ounce of you
The way you pour
your heart out there's no way
I would ever spill
your love down the drain
You've exposed
your most delicate parts
to me and you deserve
to be consumed slowly
and appreciated thoroughly

Piece Forty-eight

Thank you for being
Bold enough to love me
When the others were too afraid
To embrace my affection

Piece Forty-nine

My soul survived the dark chaos
then found you.
The light at the end of the tunnel
I once dwelled in.
You showed me what it's like to trust again
so, I gave my hand to you
knowing you'd guide us in the right direction
Not once I felt lost with you
your gift of making a heart feel at ease
is why I was willing to let go of all fears,
and follow you.
Thanks for leading me to a new life,
thanks for giving me the love
I prayed to the heavens for

Piece fifty

Reasons why I'm winning
You support the dream
without a doubt in the world
The fire that burns within in me
burns inside you too.
My twin flame
We share the same passion

You listen to my heart more than any song.
When the voice of my heartbeat sings in your
ear, you feel the soul in every word. You deeply
innerstand me dear.

We can both watch the office and laugh at the
same parts.

You're determined to never hurt me. The mirror
of trust is clear. Fear, doubt, and insecurities
disappear, when I stare deeply into those
dreaming eyes

You make me feel like the richest man in the
world because I'm in possession of the rarest
love.

Michael Tavon

You saw the world in me

and refused to settle for less.

You pray for me

the same way my mother does.

We can lay in silence

and still have the time of our lives
I'm warm with you, vulnerable
You make me feel powerful and beautiful
You love me for who I am
You changed my life
You're all mine

<u>Piece Fifty-one</u>

Often times our minds
Create illusions in our heads
So we live an alternate reality
To elude our real life problems
And past traumas

Piece Fifty-two

Chilly breeze, warm fire
Under a dark sky
Filled with patterns of stars
Crickets sings songs
Only they know
Trees tower over
Cuddling lovers
Drunk off booze, full off grilled foods
We smile, in the wild
Laughter brings tears to our eyes
Until they tire
Love is in the air
My hand runs through her hair
We live without a care
Alone with nature
Is the bliss we feel
We love each other wild
Our love is real

<u>Piece Fifty-three</u>

My hope was frozen
In the hole inside my chest
Suicidal thoughts, late night
Kept me away from a peaceful rest

I was surrounded by doubt
So I smoked to keep my mind clouded
When I came down
Darkness was still inside me

A change had to come
Old ways had to go
In order for me to elevate and grow

Now the old me is a ghost
Since I found a way to cope
Overcame depression
My heart is pumping with hope

Piece Fifty-four

It's like Deja vu

Loving you

We've must've done this

in the past life

Piece Fifty-five

The biggest lie mothers
tell their children is "I'm fine"

They hide their pain behind vials,
swallow their words, along with the pills
doctors prescribed
and say "I'm fine"

Mothers are superhero's
working against all odds
to provide safety and love
with the little they have
in the best way they know how
yet they lie and say 'I'm fine'

The stress of carrying a world
inside their hearts all alone
is a burden that kills them slowly
yet they lie and say "I'm fine"

When they suddenly
their family is surprised
because they spent a lifetime
saying "I'm fine"

Piece Fifty-six

Waking up every morning

with a smile on my face

makes life more peaceful

this is where I belong

It was a long travel,

but the lessons learned

on this journey

made it all worth it.

If I had the chance

to take another path

I would reject the opportunity,

because regret doesn't live

in this heart of mine

this journey was paved for me,

and I'll do it five times over

knowing it will lead me

Nirvana: Pieces of Self-Healing II

to where I am today.

I still have a long way to go,

but my mind is clear,

and my spirit is clean.

this path has made me

into an unbreakable

human filled with miles

of warm love

Piece Fifty-seven

Accountability must be instilled
in our little boys
so, they can grow
into honorable men

Too many mothers
are being left in the cold
raising children on their own

Too many sisters are left battered
staring through shattered glass
with tears in their eyes

Too many little girls are missing
from their homes

Too many women feel
like vulnerable prey in the wild
hounded by hyenas and beasts
in a place where they should feel safe

Sisters, mothers, and daughters
all live in a jungle

struggling to survive at peace,
because the men they love
refuse to protect them

So, let's raise our boys
to be better brothers
better sons,
and better lovers
as well as better men
that treat all women
with the same respect they give to the
women who love them.

Piece Fifty-eight

Continue to fight this battle
refuse to give up
by surviving this journey;
you could be saving the life
of someone who needs to hear your story
you're a hero to someone.

Piece Fifty-nine

You put it all on the table
the real you
even your friendship is
blissfully intense
It all makes sense,
people leave your world
because your heart
is too pure,
they don't know how to respond
well to that... fucking idiots
Well I'm here to say
I enjoy every piece you

Piece Sixty

Deep down in my heart
a fear resides, it's losing you

You've put me on a pedestal
that's too high,
and if I don't live up
to the vision in your mind
my ears will hear a harsh goodbye
and a thousand silent cries

I promise to give you my all,
I hope it's enough,
I hope my efforts,
matches your love
I don't want you to give up
On us

Now, when these thoughts occur
you reassure me
if self-doubt was an illness
you'd be the cure

You tell me I'm everything
you could ask for
sadly enough

Nirvana: Pieces of Self-Healing II

I've heard these words before
and that scares me

because someday
you might change
grow tired, become estranged
because you'd feel led astray;
you're the greatest thing
my heart has ever felt
I wish to share this love
with no one else

I want to provide for you
in ways a man should
I may not have it now
I'd give you the world if I could

one day
I'll have the means to provide for our family
for now, I thank you
for pushing me to best man I can be

I love you moon.
I hope you understand

Piece Sixty-one

we weren't two broken souls

searching for a fix with someone else

we weren't two lonely lovers

desperate for companionship

we were just two people

who became friends then fell in love.

I true bond formed with pure intentions

it's doesn't get better than that.

Piece Sixty-two

My love, as we grow old together
My dying wish is for me to die first
Because I refuse to live without her, again.

Piece Sixty-three

As the rope slips

Through my fingertips

During this tug of war battle with sadness

I grip tighter

When my muscles ache,

And claw the soil with my toes

Then pull with all my might

I won't crack the won't budge

I refuse to lose

I refuse to give up

<u>Piece Sixty-four</u>

The love we create
is the most beautiful form of art;
stemming from the heart
we listen to our wants,
and desires allowing our body heat
to spark the fire
that lights the dark room

I stroke my paintbrush
along your canvass
as we move to the dresser
from the mattress;
I form shapes and patterns
inside of you
the pictures we paint are so beautiful

I'm Basquiat with the stroke
you're Frida Kahlo with the colors;
together we make sweet love
that turns to masterpieces
under the covers

Piece Sixty-five

How to overcome depression? A tutorial

First, accept the fact that you're sad
And come up with a plan to move past it

Two, find what's holding you back, detach
Most of us
run to booze
Junk food
Sex with an ex
Late night partying
Or any drug of choice

The things we cling to
When we're in a bad mood
Are things that slowly kills us too

We must detach from old toxic patterns
And develop productive habits
(I.E, exercising, reading, creative ventures)

Step three: evaluate yourself
To elevate your mental health
(Some of us become toxic to ourselves without
being aware)

Have a heart to heart
With yourself
To figure out
Where you can improve
And build from there

And lastly, conclude
That it's not your fault
Somethings you can't control,
But you can overcome anything

Stop beating yourself over
Things that were meant to happen
You may not understand why,
But the universe made it that way for a reason:

Piece Sixty-six

Sometimes those closest to you
will try to clip your wings,
because they're afraid of
what you will become
once you learn how to fly on your own.

Get rid of the people
who fill your dreams
with doubt

Let go of the people
who hold onto the person you were
as you make strides to evolve
into the person you're becoming.

Often times, the people you love
will project their insecurities onto you
by coating is as 'realistic advice'
that's their way of holding you back,
because they were too afraid to
fly when they had to chance

So please, don't hold your wings
because of them
set the example
show them how to fly
by being fearless
hopefully they'll learn
how to fly too,
because of you

Piece Sixty-seven

I'd rather sit on the porch
Than watch the idiot box all day
Humans are the best entertainment

The neighborhood drunk
swerving on his bike
rambling about nothing
the couple across the street
causing a scene
because, he cheated again,
this week.

Jehovah's witness, moving door to door
I admire their persistence

Stray black cat's scavenging
for scraps and bugs
I wonder do black cats ever have a home

The clouds and that ball of heat and light
are both gorgeous
planes in the sky
leaving chemical trails

Most lawns are covered
with dead grass and trash

Michael Tavon

a patrol car slowly creeps down the street.

Humans are better than TV,
but where are the kids,
do they still come outside?
and why do we waste money on cable?

Piece Sixty-eight

When you're feeling low
I'm here use my strength
To life you up
I promise, heartbreak
Will never touch you again

Piece Sixty-nine

The greatest trick my mind ever played
was convincing me that I was alone
I closed my heart to those who loved me
while chasing the people who
kept me as an afterthought.
Conflicted, my mind and heart
were at war
fighting between what my heart
wanted and what my soul needed.
When confusion and chaos
killed each other off
and the dust cleared
the bloodstained surface
I was able to clearly see that the love
I desperately fought for
was close to me from the start.

Piece Seventy

misery doesn't fit in my schedule anymore
now he's jealous because
I chose to add happiness
in the time slots
where we used to spend
our quality time
he's the old friend
I used to cling to
when I felt alone
now our lifestyles don't coincide

I'm too busy growing
I'm too busy learning
I'm too busy expanding my love

misery only enjoys my company
when it's convenient for him,
and I refuse to apologize
 for choosing my light over his darkness

now misery is out somewhere
looking for a new friend to drain
all in all, I hope he finds peace soon,
because no one deserves to be held back
by his pain.

Piece Seventy-one

Even when surrounded by darkness
Choose the sliver of light
That life provides to guide your way out

You may be lost now
Hope may have left your heart
summers ago,
but you still have a chance
to be free again

Follow the light
Take your time
Never rush your blessings
You'll be fine
You'll be home again

<u>Piece Seventy-two</u>

Numb is the new happy
Bitter is the new strong
Toxic is the new love

I guess I'm too sad, weak, and functional
to understand why people my age
like to associate destructive behavior
with positive emotions.

Piece Seventy-three

I'm not bitter towards losing you because
life has been sweet since you left.

Piece Seventy-four

I cremate the broken promises

of past lovers and discard them in an urn

labeled "forgive but don't forget"

So, they can be kept safe in a place

Where they can't deceive my heart anymore

Piece Seventy-five

She finds my awkward moments cute
she just smiles and cheer
when I sing and dance
to my favorite songs in front of her.

I'm my purest self with her
Her presence gives the same comfort
I have when I'm alone with myself.

Other women tried to confine me inside
the cage of their 'standards',
but she set me free
allowing my wings to spread
in all their glory

I'm so free with her
I finally know what's it's like
to love with the same freedom
an eagle has when it soars over mountains

Piece Seventy-six

Being with her helps me forget
Everyone who took my heart
For a joyride until the tires wore out
I wasn't equipped
For heavy usage,
But they misused me
Until I broke down
They left me feeling worthless
Then she arrived, refueled my drive
Now my heart races
220 miles per hour
When she steers the wheel
And it feels so damn good
She handles me with care
And without fear
The balance my engine always needed

Piece Seventy-seven

Here are my deep dumb beautiful vulnerable
thoughts
For those who think I am well put together

I dance with self-doubt
Three times a night
Struggling to keep pace
"Am I good enough"
 "Am I on beat"
Are the thoughts
ping ponging through my head
As I try to keep up with the rhythm of life
With my two left feet
Until embarrassment eclipses my ego
And I sit down to have a deep talk with myself
These conversations typically don't go well

After that I visit my bank account
Where It's dark and vacant t
The last few dollars are holding on for dear life
I put them out of their misery
Because saving them would be a waste of time.

And at night I watch the films
 my mind plays,
They make Stephen King
seem like Nicolas Sparks
Yes, they get that dark

So, am I put well together?
Hell no, but I'm trying
To better myself day by day

Piece Seventy-eight

The same place we were born in

Is the same place we go to die

I avoid at this place at all costs

Because it's cold, expensive beyond belief,

And there's no guarantee

I'll make it out alive, even if I survive

I might leave an addict,

Or with an illness I never had

So I'll pass on every appointment and visit

I'd rather die on my own terms

Piece Seventy-nine

The first night I snored on her breasts, as her hair draped over my forehead, I discovered a comfort that helped me dream peacefully. I felt so safe in her tenderness. Her smile was so powerful I felt it through the skin of my closed eyelids. She smelled so damn good. That moment felt better than the dream I was having.

She often recalls that moment, laughing at my loud snore, and how adorable I was. My heavy head crushed her chest, but she didn't mind. My snore rattled her ears, but she didn't mind. She was just happy to feel my warmth on her chest, no matter how heavy my big ass head was weighing down on her.

Sara, I love you.

Piece Seventy-eight

Your love was made especially for me, you were the missing piece to the complicated puzzle of my heart. Now, the picture is complete, and my love is on full display for the world to see. I'm not ashamed to show; I'm not shy when it comes to telling world how happy your affection makes me. Our connection is powerful enough to inspire a world of lost hope and cynicism. You complete me, I complete you. Now let's inspire the world to love again

Piece Seventy-nine

Rest your head on my chest when you're sleeping, so you can feel how crazy my heart is for you while you're dreaming.

Piece Eighty

since saving myself from drowning

in the deep dark sea of sadness

I swam to the top

now I'm surfing on the wave of joy

bliss splashing all over my body

I smile as the wind kisses me

I've escaped the dark waters

to see the clear haven above

I'm a survivor of pain

I'm a survivor of love lost

I'm a survivor of major setbacks

I'm a survivor of broken dreams

now I bask in the ambiance of happiness

I let the cool water splash my face

I'm in a better place

all because I refused to give up

Piece Eighty-one

I grab happiness by the horns,
and laugh in its attempt
to knock me off its back

I'm a powerful force
unmovable when motivated
I refuse to lose now
I refuse to lose again

I love the feeling of joy too much
to let the gravel break my smile
when I fall
as it did once before

I'm stronger than ever
this bull won't outlast my stamina
this joy ride is going to last a lifetime

Piece Eighty-two

The world still has plenty of good left

We just gotta trudge through the mud

Shovel up every inch,

then toss the rocks to the side

to get to it.

The trouble will be worth the reward;

Because we always gotta fight for what's good.

Piece Eighty-three

the first two lessons learned
throughout childhood were
"Keep your hands to yourself"
"Treat others how you want to be treated"
Simple philosophies on how to be
a decent human being,
but as innocent boys grow older
they become entitled assholes

They touch and grope
As they please
disregarding all consequences,
because society has taught them
that it's never their fault

Society says
Rape is fine
if the woman's clothes
are too tight
Or if she waved hi
Or cracked a smile

Assault is just a figment of
a woman's exaggerated imagination

Michael Tavon

"She can't change her mind"
"Women don't know what they want"

men go to museums knowing
they can't touch the exhibits without permission,
but can't give women the same courtesy, why?

Predators are never held accountable
for their predatory ways,
women get blamed for the mistakes
their abusers make.

Piece Eighty-four

You say I've changed
Well, thanks for noticing
I used to be your puppet
Now I stand on my own

I used to feel empty
with you
Now my heart is whole
when I'm alone

I used to be
your unconditional friend
until I realized
things were only one way

I used to be your haven
Until your poisonous touch
Became a hazard to my health

I was once everything you
wanted me to be,
but when I needed love
you became numb to my feelings

So yes
things feel strange
because I've changed
into someone less convenient for you
things will never be the same

Piece Eight-five

My heart was exhausted after years of chasing love in the dry heat to find out it was all a mirage. Nothing was real when it came to the lovers of my past. They were too afraid to embrace me, too afraid to accept my affection. My love made them uncomfortable, because they were used to being mistreated. In turn they left swifter than the memory of a dream when I wake up in the morning. They made excuses as to why they couldn't love me, not you; you came into my life untamed and inhabited, like a lioness who saw what she wanted, plotted, and went for it. You came to me with a mission. Your past was left in the rearview mirror because you only saw the future of us.

You were brave enough to love me from afar, on another coast, when local women scurried as fast as they could. You were too good to be true, I tried my best not to fall for you. For the first time in my life I put up a brick wall to protect my heart. You were too driven to let that stop you, you kept pushing and pushing until you knocked it down.

Your love, your support is more than I could ask for and you keep giving. Thank you for being bold enough to love **me**

Piece Eighty-six

(To a past lover)
You didn't see my worth
I was your second choice
Now, you see my love dawned
Upon another woman
You see what you could've had
The sensation in your fingertips
have gone numb,
because you can't touch me any more
You missed what you could've had
There's no going back
You had your chance

Piece Eighty-seven

Betrayal left many scars
On the skin of your trust
It makes you feel ugly
Less worthy
Now you cry, sharing your bed with misery
And loneliness
Drowning in the thoughts of pain
Until you can no longer breath
Beating yourself up over the mistakes
Old friends and lovers made
It's not your fault
Your only mistake was falling for
strawberry smiles
hiding behind sour souls
Your love for the world
And everything in it
Makes you care with more passion
And transparency
Than your peers, my dear
It's clear to see
You can't save everyone
So why continue to hurt yourself
For people who don't have
the desire to be healed

Piece Eight-eight

A long line of rejection

led me to you

I thank those who overlooked me

For blessing me with the chance

To innerstand you

Piece Eight-nine

Every afternoon
I work with children

Some autistic
Mild or with rage
for $9 an hour
I wasn't trained
to deal with this Shit

Some have
self-esteem issues
Emotional trauma
Smart mouths
Or dumb as a box of rocks

There'd children with
ADD
Hooked on meds
Slow motor skills
Hard to play with the other kids
I gotta to manage these kids
For $9 an hour
I wasn't trained to deal with this shit

Five days a week
I'm a teacher
Tutor

Michael Tavon

PE Coach
Therapist
Anger Management Counselor
Big Brother
Father
All for $9 per hour
I wasn't trained for this shit

My back is sore
My knees ache
My head throbs too
All for $9 an hour
What a damn scam

Piece Ninety

There's a land we all know
and love
a land where dreams are made
and deferred
the animals are more civilized
than the people
love is hated, and we praise evil

"We're all created equal"
the biggest lie ever told
freedom comes with a price
only 3% can afford
where we go to war with other countries
while fighting the war in our back yard

This toxic dump
where most of us
have become numb
to it all
with drugs or alcohol
to kill our youth
getting colder and older
because it's unbearable to live here sober
the country I'm reluctant to leave
the country that's crazy enough for me
Welcome to America

Piece Ninety-one

The other women ran away from my love
They were afraid, to fall into my arms,
'cause A piece of them knew
my heart was too deep, delicate, and intense
without knowing
They protected my heart
by not falling for me too
Out of fear they shut me out
And fled the plain
Then came you
a woman who stood in front of me fearlessly
Willing to fall backwards into my arms
Unsure if I would catch you
And I did
The greatest decision
I ever made was catching you
I will never let you fall
—-You were brave enough to love me
After I was stranded in the wild
So, I refused to be the fool
who was too cowardly
to open to you
I'm here, I'm yours
Just like you, I'm all in

Piece Ninety-three

We're going to create a new universe together.
That's how deep our love is

Piece Ninety-four

You saved me from misery
A debt my heart will pay off
Until my soul retires

Piece Ninety-five

It wasn't until I learned how to love myself that
I was able to find love with someone else.

Piece Ninety-six

My desire to explore the world with you
Is boundless like the love we share
Fear is nonexistent
I'm my bravest when with you

I'm ready to embark
The most beautiful adventure
The world has ever known

Our journey will inspire movies
And love songs for years to come

The world will fall in love with us
Because what we have is that special

What we share makes Mother Nature proud
You can hear her joy when laughter

Within the crashing passion of a water fall
Even Father Time enjoys the moments we share
this is why time seems to move slow
When we make love

<u>Piece Ninety-seven</u>

My wings are finally free

I feel the breeze between my feathers

As I soar high

And low

There's no limit as to how far I can go

I can fly with my friends

I can fly alone

A bird in a cage

I am no more

Michael Tavon

Piece Ninety-eight

Tonight I'm going take your soul
By staring into those deep brown eyes
As I stroke inside of you
Then I gently grab your neck
And kiss those soft cherry lips
And say ' I love you, you're mine forever"
My motion gets deeper
Slower and deeper
You beg for more
And I give you my all
"It's yours baby, it's all yours"
Your body begins to shake
Like thunder
Then you rain all over me
Screaming my name
In many ways
Making the walls crack
Then I steal your breath away
With a single kiss

<u>Piece Ninety-nine</u>

My universe is so much more
Beautiful with you in it.
And I'm eager to explore
Beyond the surface
expose me to mountains of joy
And oceans of pleasure
Let's get lost in the jungle of wonder
And find ourselves
Making love under the maple trees
You and I
Is all the company we need
Let's fall asleep under the stars
As the moon watches over us
Then wake up to the suns bright smile
Nature seems to be in sync with us
I'm ready to explore it all
The hills, the plains, the clouds, the galaxies
Traces of our love
Will be left in every place we travel
For centuries to come

My world is so much more beautiful because of you

Piece One hundred

To new beginnings

To the life I deserve

To the life that eluded my grasps

My entire adulthood

It's finally here, in my palms

And it feels softer than I imagined

I dreamt of this life so often

It became an illusion

"No way it's real," I would say to myself

And now it's here in my hands

A genuine smile spreads across my face

This life is happiness

This life is peace, this life is love

I no longer have to dream

to feel this good

Happiness is finally my reality

Piece One hundred-one

My journey was paved especially for me
I'm fine with being misunderstood
All I need is love and support
Negative thoughts from others
And doubts from my own thoughts
Will be tuned out
I refuse to listen to anyone
that's trying to hold me back, even myself

Piece One hundred-two

He got his heart broken in so many ways
He lost himself trying to find the scattered
pieces
That could mend it back together
Everywhere he searched was darker
Than the thoughts that crowded his mind
At night
The heartache was so tragic
He came to the conclusion
That living with a fragmented heart
Was better than trying to heal the pain
altogether
He gave up on love
Until the right woman came along
And taught him
How to trust again
She slowly broke down the wall
He built to guard his broken heart
Through her
He learned he wasn't impossible to love
He learned his worth
He learned to fix heart
With her love
Without breaking her down

<u>Piece One hundred-two</u>

Her support makes me feel a like superhero
walking through a room of flying bullets
I was strong without her,
but she makes me feel invincible.

Her smile makes me forget
what heartbreak feels like
I was never broken,
but she makes me feel whole again

Her encouragement makes
my dreams more vivid
She believes in me
when I doubt myself

Her warmth makes reality
less cold
in a world where compassion
is dying
She reminds me that's there's still
some good left in it

Her love is the best
I'm so happy she gives it to me

Piece One hundred-three

Alcohol may wash
Your emotions away,
But it won't drown your sorrows
Pain killers will numb you physically,
But the pain inside will still be felt
Weed will help you forget your troubles,
But once the high fades
Those clouded thoughts
Turn into chaos
Leaving you lost
Easy sex will give an immediate release,
But once your lover leaves
Loneliness comes back to rest in your bed
Leaving you more miserable than before
No matter what vice you choose
your pain will never leave
Your mistakes will be part of you
that's nothing to be ashamed of

Piece One hundred-four

Let's envision a society
That's free of judgement
Allowing all people
To live free and the without fear
Of being killed for who they are

The society loves abundantly
With empathy and compassion
And common lies such as
"All men are created equal"
"Liberty and justice for all"
Would finally live up to their promises.

That's the world I want to live in

Piece One hundred-five

I remember when I used to stress about not receiving the support I thought I deserved. It took a while for me to realize how detrimental it was to my art and mental health. A lot of us struggle with this. Seeking validation from others comes from a deep-rooted insecurity that a lot of us share. When you don't truly believe in yourself, you want others to do it for you. Once I stopped seeking validation I refocused that energy on my craft then the support came.

Moral: people will believe in you when they can feel the confidence oozing from your pores. *Shine without shame, create without fear*

<u>Piece One hundred-five</u>

Caterpillars never complain
about being slept on
instead, they carry on stress free
Go in hiding
Evolve when no one is watching
a valuable lesson can be learned
From these little critters
Instead of stressing to impress
The world
Take advantage of the time
No one is watching
Master yourself in peace

Piece One hundred-six

In a world where people are quicker

To kick you when you're down

instead of lifting you up,

you must build a wall of confidence

made of bricks and steel,

making it impossible for negative energy to

penetrate through.

Stop seeking validation

from those,

who weren't helping you build

from the beginning

Because they are likely to pull you down

when you come up

people don't give a fuck

About you when you're struggling

With that said,

Stop wasting time trying to

Impress, the irrelevant

And take that time to grow, alone

Piece One hundred-seven

(unfinished)

So many children are born
into homes without hope
to parents who are void of love
These children get abused until
their hearts grow emotionally numb
Lack of funds, and trust
No education,
they become mentally dumb
Malnourished & neglected
Their growth, stunted
They're born with nothing

Piece One hundred-eight

Why are good people always misunderstood
and taken for granted?
Have we found such comfort in hell that love
has become something we're afraid to feel?
good people seem to suffer more
And die young
I guess, good people carry the burden of trying
to save the world
From the people who are trying to kill it
It's unfair, the world doesn't care
about the do-gooders
 until they're lying in a coffin.
That's when the flowers are given
And the tears shower
Good people are missed when dead.
But treated like shit when breathing

Michael Tavon

<u>Piece One hundred-nine</u>

Sometimes we tend mold our love interest into
an image they can't portray, because that's not
who they are. Sometimes we fantasize over the
idea of love and end up falling for someone who
isn't for us. We often fall in love with someone's
potential whist being blinded to who they really
are. Sometimes we envision an entire future
with this lover before giving them a chance to
show us who they are in the present reality. You
must learn that leading with your imagination
results in a broken heart 1000% of the time.

Piece One hundred ten

Sometimes you gotta live a day in the darkness
to appreciate the little light that you do have.

Piece One hundred eleven

Why do artists become more famous after
death?
I have a feeling that's gonna be my fate
people who could've supported me while I was
breathing will buy all my books and say,
"Damn, he was one of the greats. Had so much
to give"
Celebs coming out the woodworks to comment
"RIP 🙁" on my most recent Instagram post.
Endless photos and reviews of my works
From people who kept their support silent.
It's sucks how a lot of us are ignored when
when we're alive, but admired after we die.

Peace & Love

Michael Tavon

Thank you for reading my *Nirvana vol.2*. I would greatly appreciate if you would leave your thoughts and feelings in a brief review on amazon, Bn.com, or goodreads. Feel free to leave a massage via social media or tweet me @Michaeltavon . You may also tag me in pictures of my book(s) or your favorite pieces on Instagram @bymicaheltavon. All feedback is appreciated. Thanks for your support.

<u>Other Books</u>

(Fiction)

God is a Woman
Far from Heaven
Garage Band: The Legend of Dookie Harris
From a Cold Dark Place

(Poetry)

Songs for Each Mood vol.1
Handle with Care
Nirvana: Pieces of Self-Healing vol.1
Love & Other Things
A Day Without Sun

<u>Music</u>

Search Michael Tavon on your favorite

streaming service. Yes, I have actual music

Printed in Poland
by Amazon Fulfillment
Poland Sp. z o.o., Wrocław

49907522R00085